MULTICULTURAL CRAFTS

Exploring Native American Cultures Through Crafts

Mia Farrell

Enslow Publishing
101 W. 23rd Street
Suite 240
New York, NY 10011
USA

enslow.com

Published in 2016 by Enslow Publishing, LLC.
101 W. 23rd Street, Suite 240, New York, NY 10011

Cataloging-in-Publication Data
Farrell, Mia.
Exploring Native American cultures through crafts / by Mia Farrell.
p. cm. — (Multicultural crafts)
Includes bibliographical references and index.
ISBN 978-0-7660-6787-5 (library binding)
ISBN 978-0-7660-6785-1 (pbk.)
ISBN 978-0-7660-6786-8 (6-pack)
1. Indian craft — Juvenile literature. 2. Indians of North America — United States — Juvenile literature. 3. Handicraft —Juvenile literature. I. Title.
TT23.F377 2016
745.5089'97—d23

Printed in the United States of America

To Our Readers: We have done our best to make sure all Web site addresses in this book were active and appropriate when we went to press. However, the author and the publisher have no control over and assume no liability for the material available on those Web sites or on any Web sites they may link to. Any comments or suggestions can be sent by e-mail to customerservice@enslow.com.

Portions of this book originally appeared in the book *American Indian Crafts Kids Can Do!* by Carol Gnojewski.

Photo Credits: Crafts prepared by June Ponte; craft photography by Lindsay Pries. Andra Simionescu/Digital Vision Vectors/Getty Images (background throughout book); © AP Images, p. 20; Edward Fielding/Shutterstock.com, p. 14; Ernest Manewal/Lonely Planet Images/Getty Images, p. 8; John Cancalosi/Photolibrary/Getty Images, p. 4; Lawrence Migdale/Science Source/Getty Images, p. 22; Michael Wheatley/All Canada Photos/Getty Images, p. 10; Marilyn Angel Wynn/Nativestock/Getty Images, pp. 16, 24; mileswork/Shutterstock.com, p. 1 (Earth icon); Nativestock.com/Marilyn Angel Wynn/Nativestock/Getty Images, p. 6; Nativestock.com/Marilyn Angel Wynn/The Image Bank/Getty Images, pp. 12, 18; Rob Castro/Moment Open/Getty Images, p. 5.

Cover Credits: Crafts prepared by June Ponte; craft photography by Lindsay Pries. Andra Simionescu/Digital Vision Vectors/Getty Images (background); mileswork/Shutterstock.com, p. 1 (Earth icon).

CONTENTS

Safety Note: *Be sure to ask for help from an adult, if needed, to complete these crafts!*

Native American Cultures and Crafts

Play was an important part of life for the Native Americans of North America. Toys were not just for entertainment, but were also used to teach survival skills and history. Toy boats, toy homes, and toy weapons were just smaller versions of the real items. Playing with them helped children understand how they were made. It also helped them to develop the muscles they needed to handle them with skill.

The Southwestern Hopi tribe used Katchina dolls to teach children about katsinas, gods who bring the rain and act as messengers between humans and the spirits. Stories passed down using string games or drawing games also taught children about traditional ways of life.

A Hopi girl is dressed in traditional clothing and makeup.

Hopi Katchina dolls are created to teach children about their heritage.

But of course, there were toys that were just for fun! Native Americans from the Arctic made bull-roarers which produced loud noises. There were also board games that involved elements of luck and chance.

Each tribe may have had unique toys and games, though games were often shared as tribes met to trade and to learn from each other. Some of their toys, such as dolls, balls, and toy animals, are still played with today.

Learn and have fun as you explore the different Native American cultures of North America by crafting and playing the games in this book.

DANCING PINE DOLL FROM THE OJIBWA

The Ojibwa live in the United States and Canada. Young women of the tribe near the Great Lakes picked pine boughs from evergreen trees to craft fringy pine dolls. You can make one from feathers.

A mother and daughter are dressed in traditional Ojibwa clothing.

WHAT YOU WILL NEED

- ◎ scissors
- ◎ craft feathers
- ◎ pony bead
- ◎ ribbon

- ◎ colored pencils (optional)
- ◎ paper (optional)
- ◎ white glue

- ◎ pipe cleaner
- ◎ toilet paper tube
- ◎ wood grain contact paper
- ◎ plate or cookie tray

1. Cut three or four craft feathers of the same length. Push the feather ends through a pony bead. Trim the bottom of the feathers so that they are even. Tie a ribbon around the middle.

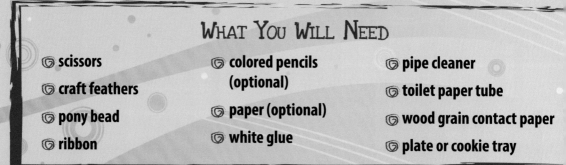

6

2. If you wish, draw a small face and neck on a piece of paper with colored pencils. Cut it out.

3. Glue the face onto the top of the feathers, over the pony bead. Twist a piece of pipe cleaner to form arms.

4. Cover a toilet paper tube with wood grain contact paper. Glue the doll to the tube. Stand your pine dancer doll on a plate (or cookie tray) and gently jiggle the plate (or tray). The dancer will appear to sway.

ILLUSTRATED STORY FROM THE YUP'IK

The Yup'ik live in Alaska. Children practice yaaruin, or illustrated stories used to help remember and share tribal traditions and values. Yup'ik girls illustrate the stories with symbols they carve into the mud or snow. The symbols would be crossed out or scraped away as the story was told.

This is a modern-day Yup'ik village in Togiak, Alaska.

WHAT YOU WILL NEED

- construction paper
- dark-colored crayons
- toothpick
- ribbon (optional)
- glue (optional)

1. Completely cover a light colored piece of construction paper with dark crayon. Press hard and add multiple layers of crayon until the surface is thick and shiny.

2. Use a toothpick to draw or scratch pictures in the crayon wax as you tell a story.

3. Glue a ribbon on the top, and your story is ready for display!

COLORFUL STICK GAME FROM THE HAIDA

The Haida, from the northwest coast of Alaska, carved cedar trees into canoes, boxes, rattles, masks, and totem poles. The Haida Painted Stick Game was played using forty to sixty finely carved and painted cedar sticks that were used similarly to playing cards.

Totem poles can be symbols for families, tribes, or individuals. Each animal has a different meaning.

Use markers or poster paint to decorate twenty-four craft sticks. The last stick can be painted in stripes or left undecorated. This is the djil, or bait. Let the sticks dry.

2. For game rules, see page 27.

CRADLEBOARD CRAFT FROM THE KIOWA

The Kiowa were originally from the northwest near the Columbia River, but they migrated to Montana before settling Oklahoma and Texas. Cradleboards were used to help carry babies. Kiowa wrapped their infants in decorated hide bags stuffed with soft dry grasses. The bag was then attached to boards that could be strapped to the back, leaned against a tree, or tied to a saddle.

Babies traveled comfortably cradleboards.

WHAT YOU WILL NEED

- empty tissue box
- hole punch
- yarn
- white glue
- 2 paint stirrers

- beads (optional)
- craft feathers (optional)
- colored toothpicks (optional)

- fabric (optional)
- straw (optional)
- a doll or stuffed animal (optional)

1. Place the tissue box vertically. Use a hole punch to punch four holes on each side of the oval opening. Lace yarn through the holes, starting from the bottom.

2. Turn the box over. Glue the two paint stirrers in a V-shape on the back. The ends of the "V" should jut out evenly at the top of the box. Let dry.

3. Decorate the area near the opening with beads or craft feathers. Or arrange varying lengths of colored toothpicks in patterns. Line the inside of the box with soft fabric or straw. Place a doll or stuffed animal inside and lace to secure.

Triangle Toy From the Penobscot

The Penobscot peeled the outer bark from the birch tree, which grew in the northeastern forests where they lived. By softening the bark in warm water, they could bend and sew it like cloth to make canoes, house coverings, food containers, musical instruments, sleds, and toys.

A birch bark wigwam is a traditional Penobscot home.

What You Will Need

- scissors
- cardboard
- pencil
- puff paint (optional)
- white or wood-grained contact paper (optional)
- aluminium foil
- ruler
- string

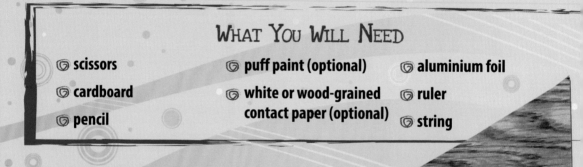

1. Use scissors to cut a piece of cardboard into an 8-inch (20-cm) equilateral triangle. (See page 26 for the pattern.) Draw a 3-inch (8-cm) circle in the middle of the triangle. Carefully cut out the circle. Cover the cardboard with white or wood-grained contact paper.

2. Crumple a piece of aluminium foil into a ball that is no more than 2 inches (5 cm) in diameter. It must be able to pass through the hole in the cardboard triangle.

3. Cut a 12-inch (30-cm) length of string. Tie one end of string around the middle of the foil ball.

4. Decorate the triangle with puff paint. Use the pointed end of the scissors to carefully poke a small hole near one corner of the triangle. Slip the other end of the string through the hole and tie it. See page 28 for game rules.

15

CORNCOB DART GAME FROM THE ZUNI

The Zuni live in New Mexico. Corn was an important crop for them, and each December, they celebrated with a ceremony for the Corn Maiden spirits, who they believed introduced corn to their people. Zuni children played a throwing game using hoops made from corn husks and darts made with dried corncobs.

Ancient Zuni petroglyphs can be found across the southwestern United States.

WHAT YOU WILL NEED

- yellow poster paint
- plastic tray
- ear of fresh or dried corn, husks removed
- construction paper
- scissors
- paper towel tubes
- white glue
- craft feathers
- hula-hoop

1. To make the darts, pour yellow poster paint into a shallow plastic tray. Roll the ear of corn in the paint and use it as a stamp to make corn kernel patterns on the construction paper. Let dry.

2. Cut the paper towel tubes in half. Glue the painted construction paper onto the cut tubes. Glue or tape feathers inside one end of each tube.

3. Grab a hula-hoop and get ready to play! For game rules, see page 28.

Cup and Pin Game From the Cree

The Chippewa-Cree lived in the sub-arctic before migrating to Montana. Children used shells or cone-shaped bones to make this version of a ring and pin game. Playing this game taught coordination skills helpful for spearing fish and other animals.

Chippewa-Cree dancers perform at a powwow, or gathering, in Montana.

What You Will Need

- white glue
- crepe paper
- small paper cup

- scissors
- pipe cleaners
- beads

- yarn
- unsharpened pencil
- clear tape

1. Glue crepe paper around the cup, and trim. Add pipe cleaners and beads.

2. Carefully poke a small hole in the bottom of the cup.

3. Thread a 3-foot (1-m) length of yarn through the hole so that the rim of the cup faces downward. Tie a knot at the top end of the yarn so the cup does not fall off.

4. Tie an unsharpened pencil at the bottom end of the string and secure with tape. To play the game, hold the pencil upright. Swing the cup up and away from you. Try to move the pencil so that the cup lands on it.

BANNOCK BUZZING SPIN TOY

The Bannock and the Northern Shoshone lived in the grasslands of the Great Basin and along the Snake River in Idaho. Bannock children drilled holes in flat, round animal bones or pottery pieces to make a buzzing spin toy, which works like a two-handed yo-yo.

A boy dresses up to perform a traditional dance at the Shoshone–Bannock Indian Festival.

WHAT YOU WILL NEED

- ⊚ two 1-1/4 to 1-1/2-inch (3–4 cm) metal washers
- ⊚ poster paint
- ⊚ paintbrush
- ⊚ scissors
- ⊚ cardboard
- ⊚ rubber cement
- ⊚ string or yarn

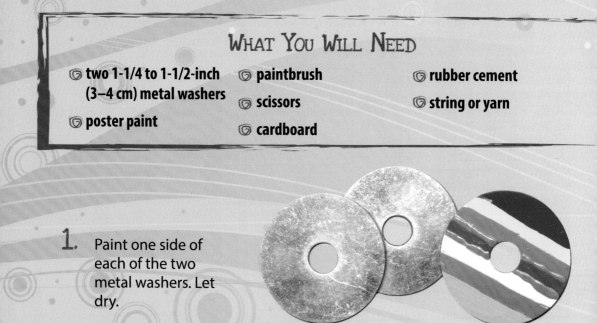

1. Paint one side of each of the two metal washers. Let dry.

2. Cut a 2-inch (5 cm) circle out of cardboard. (See page 26 for the pattern.)

4. Cut a 20- to 24-inch (50-60 cm) length of string or yarn. Thread one end of the string through one hole and the other end of the string through the second hole. Knot the ends. For instructions on how to play, see page 29.

3. With rubber cement, glue the blank sides of the washers to the left and right sides of the cardboard disk. Ask an adult to poke two holes through the center of the washers and through the cardboard. The holes should be 1/2 inch (1 cm) apart.

Marble Game From the Cherokee

Cherokee were farmers and hunters in the southeast United States. Cherokee children made marbles from clay soil, round river rocks, or pine sap. Adults chipped large stones to make marbles as big as billiard balls. They threw them at a set of holes in the ground and tried to knock other teams' marbles out of the way.

This re-creation shows what a Cherokee village might have looked like.

What You Will Need

- 🌀 hardening clay
- 🌀 poster paint
- 🌀 paintbrush
- 🌀 white glue
- 🌀 scissors
- 🌀 shoebox with lid
- 🌀 markers

1. Roll the clay into marble-sized balls. Make them as smooth and round as you can. Let the marbles air dry.

2. Paint them in bright, swirling colors. Let dry. Coat the marbles with a thin layer of white glue. This will seal the marbles and make them shiny. Let dry.

3. Carefully cut five holes slightly bigger than the marbles into the bottom half of the lid. The holes should form an L-shape. Use a marker to label the holes from one to five.

4. Lean the lid against the shoebox, and you are ready to start playing! For instructions on how to play, see page 29.

ACORN SPINNING TOP FROM THE POMO

Pomo lived in northern California. Each fall, Pomo children gathered acorns from oak trees. Acorns were a big part of their diet. They were shelled and boiled or mashed to make soup, bread, dyes, and medicines. Children played with acorns as spinning tops.

Ground acorn soup, berries, and deer meat were traditional foods of the Pomo.

WHAT YOU WILL NEED

- hardening clay
- 3-inch stick or dowel
- toothpick
- poster paint
- paintbrush
- white glue (optional)

1. Roll a chunk of clay into a 2-inch (5 cm) ball. Insert the stick (or dowel) into the center. One inch (2.5 cm) should stick out from the top.

2. For the top of the acorn, flatten a second chunk of clay into a circle. Use a toothpick to add an acornlike texture.

3. Mold the clay around the stick into a rounded triangular or acorn shape. Place the acorn cap onto the clay ball. Let the clay dry.

4. Once the clay is dry or hard, paint it acorn colors. Let dry. To make it shiny, use a thin layer of white glue. Let dry. Set the top on a flat surface. Roll the stick between your thumb and pointer finger and let go to spin it.

PATTERNS

The percentages included on the patterns tell you how much to enlarge or shrink the image using a copier. Most copiers and printers have an adjustable size/percentage feature to change the size of an image when you print it. After you print the pattern to its correct size, cut it out. Trace it onto the material listed in the craft.

Bannock Bone Buzzer

At 100%

Enlarge by 200%

Penobscot Birch Triangle Toy

Game Rules

Haida Painted Stick Game

1. This is a two-person game. The object is to locate the djil, or bait, and collect the most sticks.

2. Player One divides all of the sticks into two handfuls. He or she shuffles each handful with his or her back turned away from Player Two.

3. Player Two chooses the hand he or she believes the bait is in.

4. Player One throws that handful onto the placemat. If the bait is there, Player Two keeps all of the sticks in the pile except for the bait. Player Two then divides the remaining sticks into two handfuls and shuffles them for Player One.

5. If the bait is not there, Player Two keeps nothing. He or she divides all of the sticks into two handfuls and shuffles them for Player One.

6. Repeat until the last pile is won. Then count the sticks. The player with the most sticks wins.

PENOBSCOT BIRCH TRIANGLE TOY GAME

1. To play, grasp a corner of the triangle opposite the string side.
2. Flip up the corner, tossing the ball into the air.
3. Try to move the triangle so that the ball drops through the hole.

ZUNI CORNCOB DART GAME

1. This game is best played outside or in a big open room. Gather two or more players.
2. Have one person roll the hula-hoop along the ground or the floor.
3. As the hula-hoop rolls past, try to throw the darts through the hoop. Or try and knock the hula-hoop over with the darts.

BANNOCK BUZZING SPIN TOY

1. To play, hold one end of the string in each hand.

2. Hold the string parallel with the disk in the center. Twirl the string until it is tight. Or twirl the disk until the string is tight.

3. Then move both hands toward the disk and then quickly away as if you were playing an accordion. The disk will begin to spin.

4. Keep twirling the string and pulling away. This motion will keep the disk spinning. The weight of the washers aids the momentum of the disk.

CHEROKEE MARBLE GAME

1. Turn the shoebox over. Prop the lid against the box so that it is at a slant.

2. Choose a number from one to five. Then roll a marble down the box lid, aiming for the hole with that number.

3. Keep score if you wish. Play alone or with friends.

LEARN MORE

Freed, Kira. *Learning about Native Americans With Arts & Crafts*. New York: Powerkids Press, 2015.

Kuskowski, Alex. *Super Simple Native American Art: Fun and Easy Art from around the World*. Edina, Minn.: ABDO Publishing, 2013.

Minnesota Historical Society and Mille Lacs Indian Museum. *Ojibwe Shoulder Bag Kit*. St. Paul, Minn.: Minnesota Historical Society Press, 2013.

Yasuda, Anita. *Explore Native American Cultures! With 25 Great Projects*. White River Junction, Vt.: Nomad Press, 2013.

WEB SITES

Freekidscrafts.com/world-crafts/native-american-crafts/

Make totem poles, headdresses, and dream catchers from everyday items!

enchantedlearning.com/crafts/indian/

Create a model tepee, paper canoe, rainstick, and more!

native-languages.org/kids.htm

Learn about the different Native American tribes, including their hairstyles, clothes, food, and homes.

INDEX